SURVIVAL ZONE

# SURVIVE A TSUNAMI

BY PATRICK PERISH

TORQUE™

BELLWETHER MEDIA · MINNEAPOLIS, MN

™

Are you ready to take it to the extreme? Torque books thrust you into the action-packed world of sports, vehicles, mystery, and adventure. These books may include dirt, smoke, fire, and chilling tales. **WARNING**: read at your own risk.

Library of Congress Cataloging-in-Publication Data

Names: Perish, Patrick, author.
Title: Survive a Tsunami / by Patrick Perish.
Description: Minneapolis, MN : Bellwether Media, Inc., [2017] | Series: Torque: Survival Zone | Includes bibliographical references and index. | Audience: 007-012.
Identifiers: LCCN 2015050797 | ISBN 9781626174450 (hardcover : alk. paper)
Subjects: LCSH: Tsunamis–Juvenile literature. | Severe storms–Juvenile literature.
Classification: LCC GC221.5 .P47 2017 | DDC 613.6/9–dc23
LC record available at https://lccn.loc.gov/2015050797

Printed in the United States of America, North Mankato, MN.

# TABLE OF CONTENTS

# A DEADLY FORCE

On December 26, 2004, a powerful **earthquake** set off tsunamis around the Indian Ocean. The biggest hit Indonesia. Seven-year-old Martunis was in his family's van when the tsunami struck.

The incoming wave roared like a jet engine. It swept up everything in its path, including the van. Martunis lost sight of his mom. He would not see her again.

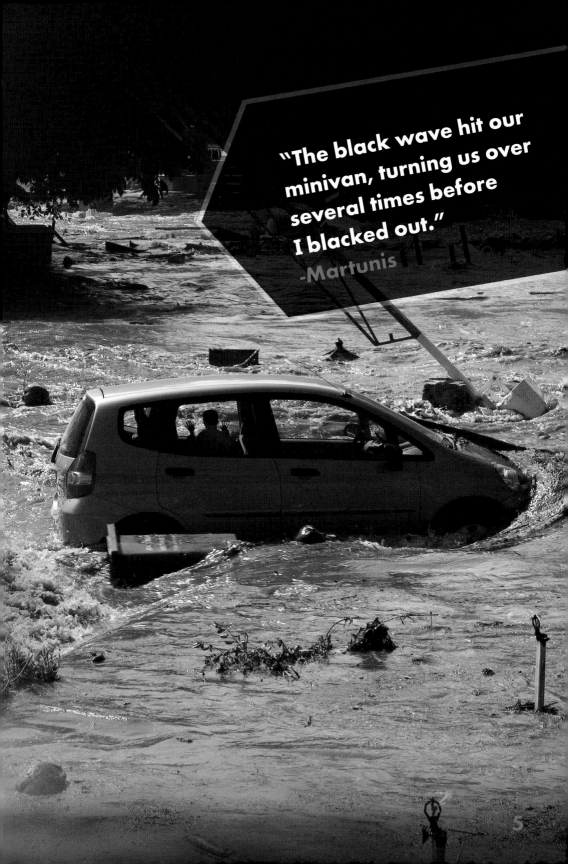

"The black wave hit our minivan, turning us over several times before I blacked out."

-Martunis

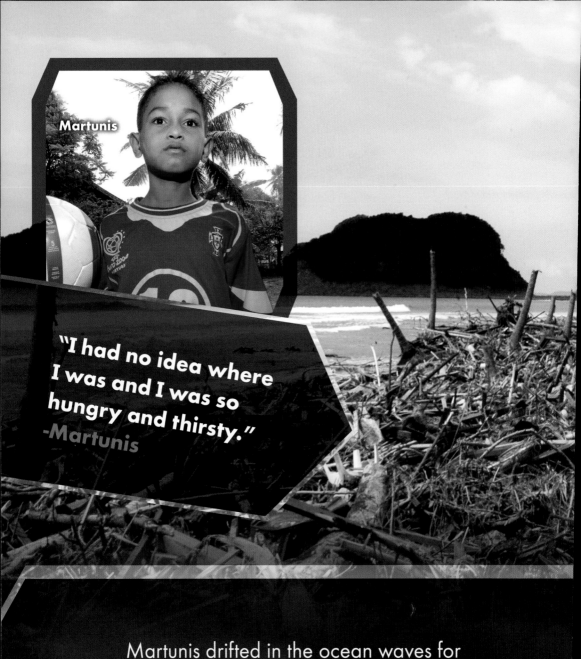

Martunis

"I had no idea where I was and I was so hungry and thirsty."
-Martunis

Martunis drifted in the ocean waves for

# BIRTH OF A TSUNAMI

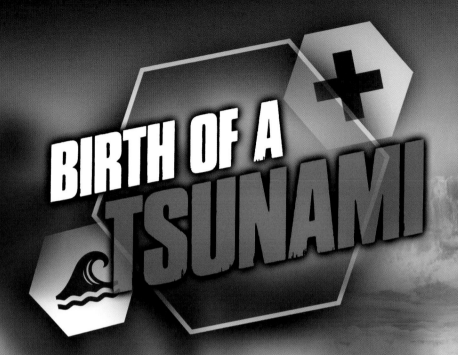

A tsunami is a series of big, powerful waves that bring destruction when they hit land. They happen when large volumes of water are suddenly **displaced**. Most are caused by earthquakes.

# TSUNAMI WARNINGS

**TSUNAMI WATCH:**
An earthquake or other similar activity has occurred. A tsunami is possible. Stay tuned for more information.

**TSUNAMI ADVISORY:**
Strong currents are likely. Widespread flooding is not expected. Stay away from shore.

**TSUNAMI WARNING:**
A tsunami is likely. Widespread flooding is expected. Listen for evacuation orders.

A tsunami forming close to shore can strike with little warning. If you live near the coast, make a plan. Know the fastest way to **evacuate** to high ground. Prepare an emergency kit.

If you feel an earthquake, listen to the radio for tsunami warnings. After long-lasting earthquakes, do not wait for a warning. You may not have much time.

# EMERGENCY KIT LIST

flashlight

emergency radio

extra batteries

dry or canned food

bottled water

first aid kit

clothing

cash

cell phone and charger

blankets

medications

road maps

Tsunamis ripple out from their **origin** at tremendous speeds. In deep water, their waves move fast but only rise a few feet. As waves approach land, they slow down and rise up until their **crests** reach staggering heights.

People caught out at sea during a tsunami warning should wait to return to harbor. They are safer out on deep water.

# HOW A TSUNAMI FORMS

**DEEP WATER:**
waves are short and
far apart

**NEAR SHORE:**
waves get closer together
and increase in height

sea level

ORIGIN:
water is displaced

## A RECORD BREAKER

The largest recorded wave
formed in a narrow bay in
Alaska. A landslide unleashed
a blast of water that
reached up to 1,720 feet
(524 meters)!

Before a tsunami, the ocean may **recede** quickly and expose the seafloor. This sudden drop in water level is a warning. Head for high ground.

Sometimes people run out to observe the seafloor. When the wave arrives, they have no time to flee. They get caught in the tsunami's **inland** rush. Some get dragged out to sea by strong receding waves.

## INCOMING!

Witnesses say an incoming tsunami sounds like a freight train.

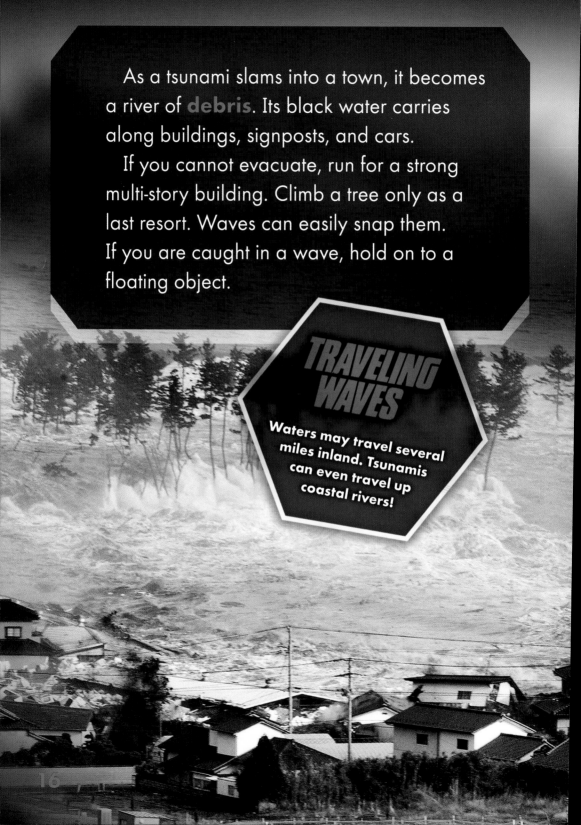

As a tsunami slams into a town, it becomes a river of **debris**. Its black water carries along buildings, signposts, and cars.

If you cannot evacuate, run for a strong multi-story building. Climb a tree only as a last resort. Waves can easily snap them. If you are caught in a wave, hold on to a floating object.

## TRAVELING WAVES

Waters may travel several miles inland. Tsunamis can even travel up coastal rivers!

# HOW HIGH CAN TSUNAMIS REACH?

Krakatoa Volcano tsunami
August 26-27, 1883
**130 feet
(40 meters)**

Indian Ocean tsunami
December 26, 2004
**100 feet
(30 meters)**

small tsunami
**10 feet
(3 meters)**

**Statue of Liberty
151.9 feet
(46.3 meters)**

**White House
60.3 feet
(18.4 meters)**

**average human
5.3 feet
(1.6 meters)**

**2011 tsunami, Tokyo**

17

# ACROSS THE WORLD

Tsunamis can travel huge distances. The 1960 earthquake near Chile caused tsunamis in Japan!

After a wave recedes, do not return to the shore. A tsunami is made up of many waves. The second wave can be even bigger than the first.

Waves may continue to hit the coast for hours. Return home only when authorities tell you it is safe.

# AFTER THE TSUNAMI

Tsunami cleanup can be long and dangerous. Buildings damaged by floodwaters may **collapse** at any moment. Stay clear of downed power lines and any debris. Avoid drinking faucet water until officials consider it safe. With good planning and fair warning, you can survive a tsunami!

# TSUNAMI RISK AROUND THE WORLD

Tsunamis can happen in any large body of water. However, some places have a larger risk than others. Earthquakes in the Pacific make it a likely place for tsunamis to begin.

high tsunami risk = █    moderate tsunami risk = ▪

low tsunami risk = ▫

**2011 Japanese tsunami cleanup**

POLICE

## THE REALLY BIG ONE

Scientists say a massive earthquake and tsunami is due to strike the northwestern United States. The last one hit in 1700.

# GLOSSARY

**collapse**—to fall apart

**crests**—the tops of waves

**debris**—the remains of something broken down or destroyed

**displaced**—forced out or moved out of position

**earthquake**—a sudden movement of Earth's crust; undersea earthquakes are the leading cause of tsunamis.

**evacuate**—to leave a dangerous area

**inland**—the part of a country away from coasts

**landslides**—masses of earth or rocks that slide down steep slopes

**meteorites**—space rocks that hit Earth

**origin**—the point or place where something begins

**recede**—to fall or pull back

**volcanoes**—holes in the earth; when a volcano erupts, hot, melted rock called lava shoots out.

# TO LEARN MORE

## AT THE LIBRARY

Larson, Kirsten. *Tsunamis*. Vero Beach, Fla.: Rourke Educational Media, 2015.

Portman, Michael. *Savage Tsunamis*. New York, N.Y.: Gareth Stevens Pub., 2012.

Swanson, Jennifer. *Tsunamis*. Minneapolis, Minn.: ABDO Publishing Company, 2014.

## ON THE WEB

Learning more about surviving a tsunami is as easy as 1, 2, 3.

1. Go to www.factsurfer.com.

2. Enter "survive a tsunami" into the search box.

3. Click the "Surf" button and you will see a list of related web sites.

With factsurfer.com, finding more information is just a click away.

# INDEX